TRENDING WITHOUT A FOLLOWING

SUCCESS IS A MUST

DARE PAUL DUROJAYE

INDIA • SINGAPORE • MALAYSIA

ISBN 979-8-89699-503-6

DEDICATION

I dedicate this book to God for making the book possible.

I also dedicate this book to everyone whose dreams and visions remain a focus. Let's go on a journey together as we unravel what's next for you.

Contents

Acknowledgement

I acknowledge my wife, Olasunkanmi Eldrida Durojaye and our sons, Oluwaferanmi Emmanuel Durojaye and Oluwanifemi Edwin Durojaye, for standing strong with me.

I also acknowledge Busayo Victor Durojaye, Co-founder of Loopify (www.tryloopify.com), for his contributions to the production of this book.

Introduction

The World Population Prospect, according to the United Nations for 2024, is 8.2 billion. It's pretty amazing how some celebrities have a chunk of the population following them on social media. These followings are then monetized. The more the following, the more your influence and this mass communication process gives a large view of products and services being pushed by manufacturing companies and others for advertisement.

Technology is advancing our space, making communication and advertisement easier by the day with its coverage to more and more people, and this is not likely to stop soon. People have lived and maximised their potential to the height of technology in their days. So here we are with the following trends on social media, which gained great traction during and after COVID-19 as that was the best means of communication since gathering in church, mosque, studio, or workplace were not allowed.

Trending is now a form of success where you are viewed by millions of people around the world. I am writing this book to underscore the language of today while passing a message of success to you in a way that shines the light on the vast potential that lies in you. I am also drawing your attention to the book of all ages, which is the Bible, to make you see what is lying fallow on your inside, what was said about it thousands of years ago, and how to activate the special potential in you for the world to see and benefit from.

To leave your footprints in the sand of time requires you to discover the capacity God put inside you and awaken it to the benefit of the world. After all, you are the light of the world. You can trend by pushing yourself to the full capacity of your potential. There is a well of potential in you meant to quench the thirst of the thirsty. There is a potential in you that must be activated to solve the problem of international trade systems, intra-African trade systems, global warming, poverty and multi-dimensional poverty, education and parenting. The list goes on and on, and the world is waiting for you to bring your gifts to bare.

If you are able to read this book to the end, you would understand things you have undermined, habits you need to put away, and how to take the necessary steps going forward. It will surprise you how easy it is to activate the gifts you have and make them benefit your immediate environment. Sometimes, money is not the goal, but the truth is when there is a flow of potential, there is also the flow of money because money is a current that must flow. The next page promises to show you how to start the success journey.

Part 1

LAYING THE FOUNDATIONS

Chapter 1

Assessing Your Environment

"Now there is in Jerusalem by the Sheep Gate a pool in Hebrew called Beth-zatha, which has five porticoes. In these lay a multitude of invalids, blind, lame, paralysed"

– (John 5:2-3)

Your present state could easily be identified by the flock of people around you. Changing your status by changing your mind must be driven by dreams and visions. These dreams and visions must eventually transform you into a new environment of people of like minds. The fruit is never far-fetched from the tree. Change is inevitable, good or bad. The possibility of a higher status, self-realisation in finance, business or marriage is achieved in phases and the people around you for each phase must reflect where you are going.

Flocking at your level is one thing; aspiring to another level is better. You must realise that you can easily determine your status or state at a particular moment by looking at the people you are surrounded with, including books and what you pay attention to online. David was a friend to Jonathan, who was the son of a king at that time. Guess what? David was in line to be the next king.

An unnamed paralysed man was said to be in the company of like minds in Jerusalem. Associations can seem trivial but their impact is usually enormous in nature. If you are a Christian, it's good to have Christian friends, but note that you will never be more than the environment and associations you are locked in. There must be value to friendship. You must make progress in life; if not, who are your friends or the association you keep? Friendship can activate new levels of wealth, IQ, and ease of living in achieving purpose and not just discussing people or events. Friendship should probably be based on purpose. It should be about where you are heading, so if you don't know or have a place you are going in life, you will most likely be in the company of the same.

Billionaires are friends with billionaires, inventors are friends with investors, and geniuses are friends with geniuses. Who is your friend? Sometimes, there are no friends or people you can call friends. This could be because you have left them due to a higher purpose, or they have left you because you are still lagging behind. There is a period when all the people you call friends are gone. Everyone has moved on with life in different directions. Those who are with you are probably going in the same direction as you. This happens to everyone, and it works itself out with or without your awareness. Movement consciousness is a sign of good living. Movement is not necessarily by location in the geographical sphere but movement in terms of career, purpose and the likes. Iron sharpens iron (Proverbs 27:17), so I'm wondering at what point you became a wood that can no longer be sharpened by iron but cut. In other words, you need to know when to leave some associations because they no longer sharpen you. This is a success factor.

Say Goodbye

Assessing your environment leverages you for optimum potential attainment. It will require you to say goodbye to some associations, while to others, it is welcome. I am not suggesting that friendship should be based on what's in it for you. Friendship should be about love and care. Love and care will bring about new dimensions to friendships in ways that will make living better for each other.

While assessing your environment and some associations fall short of the next phase of your life, especially when there is a pullback at every attempt to reach the next phase, saying goodbye is not a crime. Unfortunately, some associations just dissolve automatically, while others need a conscious effort to detach yourself from what is not progressive to your destiny.

In local palace, "20 kids cannot play together for 20 years". This is true because destiny calls each one of us as we grow. Healthy friendships and associations are as good for destiny as healthy foods are for the body.

More often than not, we don't want to let go of the familiar because of the time shared. Time has given space for conflicts and resolutions, memorable moments through which you have understood each other. That same process goes almost with every association because it gives room for understanding.

Destiny's call is weightier than associations not pointing you in the right direction towards the purpose of the greater good. That should be your focus and not necessarily keeping associations of talkers and not doers. Goodbye can be painful at the moment, but it will subside with time. You were not created as a mannequin in a show glass. You have a purpose to fulfil in this world.

Find a Benchmark

When you know where you ought to be in purpose by design, you need to find someone who has achieved what you are aspiring to attain. That gives you leverage that what you are aspiring to achieve is definitely achievable. That is one of the benefits of association. Good association should make you doubt your doubts and not your beliefs.

Association should build your faith towards achieving your set goals, and this makes your journey in life interesting. There will be days when your soul will fret, but you will find comfort in the reality of the possibility of your dream.

It's ultimately your job to seek your benchmark, someone who has done what you are aspiring to achieve as a goal or as a vision. It is a deliberate attempt at solidifying your next steps of faith towards your goals. I will admit it is sometimes difficult to get time with such people because of their busy schedules, but your level of thirst for your goal will determine the outcome. As a matter of fact you need to get more of their books or podcast online and listen to them over and over again. It's about how bad you want it. You need to develop your own blueprint for studying and/or getting the attention of the person you have chosen as your benchmark, like blind Bartimaeus, who kept screaming until he got the attention of Jesus.

Your benchmark may not necessarily be an individual; it could be an institution, organisation or association. The first motive, however, is to help your mind see where you would like to be with the intent of accomplishing your goals. This is to help you understand the terrain of the path you have chosen to follow. More often than not, it also helps you avoid the potholes that are avoidable because, in the end, you still have to carry your cross and determine how the story ends.

In spite of your failures and lost opportunities, you must always get back up again to try with a clear vision of what you intend to achieve. Age should not be your barrier, neither should disappointments be your excuse. You must be determined to say at the end, "I came, I saw and conquered." Nobody said the road would be easy, so get up on your feet and try again. Try different methods you have not used before because as life changes, so do methods. Let it be an adventure, and give room for failure, which simply means a way by which a method could not achieve your desired result. Failure, my friend, is never denial.

Failure should be seen as part of the process. The condemnation of failure during academic pursuit gives failure a completely black image, but truthfully, failure will take the colour you assign to it. Failure is a temporary setback, not a stop. So, stop beating yourself over the last attempt. You are on the right path with legends that have shaped our world. If they acknowledged failure as a defeat, maybe there wouldn't be light, aeroplanes, telecommunications, etc.

Our children should be trained with the mindset that failure is an opportunity to try again. This is crucial for high development. Stories are written and could be erased or edited to suit the intention of the writer. Likewise, failure could be erased and edited until you achieve your goal. It doesn't end until you end it. Failure is not final. This would eventually encourage you to move on in the path you have chosen, applying different concepts until success is achieved. It's not over until you say so. That's the god in you because the scripture calls us gods (Psalm 82:6). God created the world in six days and rested on the seventh day, but that doesn't mean if you try six times, it's over. You are the only one given the capacity to determine when an event in your life, career, and family is over.

I so much believe in the purpose of God for your life, do you? I admonish you to turn to the next page. I'd like to introduce to you the dynamics of consistency.

Chapter 2

The Power of Consistency

'One man was there, who had been ill for thirty-eight years'

– (John 5:5)

Achieving weight loss or muscle building is not so much about the exercise itself but how consistent you are at exercising. We often talk about this man who has been ill for thirty-eight years but fail to mention that he has been consistent on the path to healing, to liberating himself from a disreputable status. He has been ill for thirty-eight years, so I can assume he has been seeking healing for thirty-eight years or less. He could have given up on his illness and taken it as a permanent condition, but this unnamed man stood consistent, believing that one day he would enter the pool before anyone else and get his healing.

Consistency does not mean doing the same thing the same way and expecting a different result. Consistency is being steady. It is about uniformity and reliability. Consistency can be divided into internal consistency and external consistency.

Internal consistency is the coherence within a system. First, the internal coherence should be with your spirit, soul, and body. You are a spirit with a soul, living in a body. That is what makes you a human. Therefore, your spirit, soul, and body must have a constant coherence. If you are indulging in habits that don't agree with your spirit, soul, and body, your internal inconsistency will affect and influence your decisions. If the food you eat doesn't nourish your body, it will definitely show in your appearance because there is no coherence. Your spirit, soul, and body must constantly agree for you to have transformative changes in your actions. Your success story starts with you. Your coherence is vital to your success. That is the omission you have been trying to figure out. The alignment of your spirit, soul, and body is your major first step to achieving success.

When you are able to achieve this coherence within you, you are better enabled to be consistent in character, on the job, which invariably builds trust, reliability, and reduces your margin of error to the barest minimum. You won't have to wait to be appreciated because you are already in sync with yourself. You won't have to wait to be approved by someone else because you have achieved a state of balance within yourself.

External consistency is the alignment of actions, decisions, or outputs in business, education, sports, customer service, etc. External consistency could be seen in industrial standards, regulatory compliance, market expectations, social norms, and organisational policies. Brand consistency, for instance, is vital for profit and the lifespan of a product. Your uniqueness will be seen on the job and in how you relate and communicate. Holding up high standards and values, following rules and regulations will be a norm for you, and this will definitely spark reactions, both positive and negative towards you. Embrace the positive reactions while using the negative reactions as a stepping stone.

The idea is don't stop working on what you believe in. More often than not, success is predicated and achieved by people who are consistent in what they do. Consistency in integrity, love, hard work, gym, reading, keeping appointments and other important values will land you safely at your destination and possibly beyond your imagination. The journey is as important as the destination. Consider how God puts it, "if you are neither hot nor cold, I will vomit you" Rev. 3:16.

The power of consistency radiates a magnetic force that pulls strings in the universe to make things work for you. The power of consistency will attract a sponsor, divine help, or both in other instances.

A SPONSOR: I will liken a sponsor to someone who speaks on your behalf in boardrooms or with people who are not ordinarily at your reach. This is so because the sponsor must have had an encounter with you or your product, and the sponsor is convinced about your passion and what you are willing to offer.

DIVINE HELP: If a sponsor doesn't show up in literal human form, then the power of consistency will draw in the divine. We can talk about inventors and how many times they failed but never gave up until success was achieved because they were consistent. For this ill, unnamed, paralysed man of thirty-eight years, Jesus showed up as both God and man.

The power of consistency cannot be overemphasised. To get to the top of the ladder in your career needs consistency, not undermining game plans and the bureaucracy with politics that goes on. The scripture 2 Timothy 4:2 admonishes us to be consistent, ready in season and out of season.

If you have read this book to this point, it is time to understand what your thoughts can create in order for you to achieve success.

Part 2

TRANSFORMATIVE THINKING

Chapter 3

Don't Lose Sight of Other Possibilities

"When Jesus saw him and knew that he had been lying there a long time, he said to him, 'Do you want to be healed?'

– (John 5:6)

Don't allow doing what you are doing consistently to make you lose sight of new possibilities of doing things to achieve the same or better results. Change is always a constant phenomenon in life. Don't be afraid of change. Most times, change is often rejected before it is accepted. The paralysed man's only healing approach or focus was to jump into the pool. That was the only means of healing he was exposed to. Jesus asked him the question to shift his mentality to a new possibility of healing without jumping into the pool. There is always a better way.

This is fundamental to success. SpaceX launched a rocket, and the same rocket landed successfully on the same spot from which it was launched. This was deemed impossible until someone thought of other ways to make it happen. Is it possible you have given up on so many things because they didn't work; maybe it's time to change your perspective on how you are going about the process? There is always a better way. Life is full of possibilities if you can imagine it.

Flying an aircraft was once impossible. In fact, I am wondering what your impossibilities were before you read this book. It was impossible because you called it impossible. 'Do you want to be healed?' was a deliberate question to make the paralysed man see the possibility of healing in another way. He has been consistent on the path to healing, but he was only exposed to one way for 38 years and could not achieve it. Maybe your next line of action over the impossibility is to ask yourself questions that could expose your perspective and push you beyond the limit you have set in your mind.

Exposure is vital for possibilities. It gives your mind the ignition needed to pull beyond the ordinary to accomplish your desired goals, dreams, and visions. In simple terms, dreams and visions are a type of exposure you need to earn. Dreams and visions are about seeing the possibility of a thing with your hindsight, which is your imagination. Dreams and visions are not what you get while sleeping; rather, they keep you from sleeping. Beyond imagination, you need to be able to draw out the sketches of your imagination in reality. Those sketches of your imagination are unique, and for you to have them simply means it is possible to birth them. Exposure plays an important role in helping you birth your unique vision in your career, in parenting, on your job, and in every sphere of life you are involved in.

Specifically for parents, exposure cannot be overemphasised. Parents are basically the first model for children. Parents who lack of exposure can limit their children's capacity significantly in life, especially in choosing a path for their lives. Guidance is key to parenting, and that makes it important that parents have enough exposure to see ahead for their kids and not just hope they can be what they were not. It could be a big mistake to throw your child into the medical profession because you couldn't attain it or because you love it. The result you eventually get is that the child will have to struggle throughout the career's lifespan except the child finds his or her niche. You don't want to see your child struggle, but your exposure is directly linked to his or her future. Struggling is a painful experience because when the child starts to see what he or she should have become, it hurts. Time is lost. So you want to be prepared to lead and guide your child on the path that is most suitable for them to flourish.

If you are a victim of such parenting, there is still room for a shift. The best time to plant a tree was 20 years ago, and the next best time is now. Do not bask in the euphoria of blame; shift. Move to what your gifts can accomplish, write that book, compose that song, go for your master's degree. Just do what God has imprinted in your DNA for you to flourish. Your best is yet to be seen.

Exposure gives you the liberty to choose right, act right and do right in endeavours that matter. Exposure to books, important places, seminars and conferences, great men and women who are trailblazers, exposure to information on the path you have chosen will eventually help you to see better and plan better. Why waste your time when you can use that time to master the art of drawing the sketches of your imagination. Exposure and possibilities are interconnected. Your job is to get your mind ignited through the necessary exposures needed.

Perspective is everything. Exposure helps you see broader and wider. It enhances the scope of your lenses in critically dissecting issues and making decisions on a higher frequency. Misunderstandings between husbands and wives are mainly based on different perspectives. Both are speaking or standing on the truth they know through cognitive experiences, but that doesn't automatically suggest right or wrong based on the situation at hand. The degree to which you get angry and express anger is based on perspective. For more efficiency in dealing with people, you must always have a holistic view of the subject from the other person's point of view. Perspective makes you take certain decisions and actions for or against certain scenarios. You need to equip yourself with information that can help you see life from a broader perspective because that's how you can navigate pitfalls of life in marriage, in business, at work, or with associations that are beneficial to you. Destruction comes with a narrow perspective of situations. You blow things out of proportion and later regret it, but the damage has been done.

Exposure helps in expanding your perspective, which in return helps your decision-making process. You are better equipped with the understanding that in life your point of view is not the only truth. It gives you the ability to tolerate others, knowing you make errors as well and that life is not always perfect. Widen your scope through books, travelling to see other cultures. This makes you appreciate the dynamics of life that sometimes day here is night elsewhere.

Reasoning for a Living

Reasoning is the cognitive process of drawing logical conclusions from available information, evaluating arguments and making informed decisions. The cognitive process is achieved through the senses on things you have heard, seen, felt, touched or tasted. You are able to recognise something or someone you have seen before. So, recognition is from the cognitive process of what you have seen before. The brain stores things you have seen or heard in your memory and when you see it or hear it again, you could recognise or remember it. Your senses feed your mind on daily basis. This is a natural occurrence.

This should make you intentional in your daily activities because your cognitive process needs to be broad enough to think widely to make the best decisions for your children, home, business, career, and projects. You have to be intentional about your thought process. There is usually a pattern or line of processing and evaluating things due to past experiences or exposure. You need to identify your own and see the merits and demerits of your line of thought. Putting your line of thought to the test at various times to understand your pattern of cognitive process is essential for your reasoning faculty. Unknowingly, you have made certain errors of judgement based on your cognitive process, and this process will keep repeating itself if you don't check it. That's where the adage 'think twice' is applicable. Thinking twice simply means to consider your first line of thought process again and subject it to various views in your mind to see if it will pass the test of time before you turn it into an action or a decision.

The mastery of your reasoning faculty is a good sense of maturity. This is vital for the overall successes you record in your life. Not to decide is to decide because decisions are inevitable on a daily basis. These decisions, in turn, coagulate to make who you are. There are some people that won't decide on a matter and won't let others decide. Goal-getters make up their minds as to what and what not to do. Some make decisions based on emotions, which are seldom right. There is no crime in making a decision based on emotion if it is absolutely right because we all do, but there is a higher level of making decisions based on informed reasoning.

Think Limitless

"The sea rose because a strong wind was blowing. When they had rowed three or four miles, they saw Jesus walking on the sea and drawing near to the boat. They were frightened. But he said to them, 'It is I, do not be frightened.' Then they were glad to take him into the boat, and immediately the boat was at the land to which they were going"

– (John 6:18-21).

The context of the story was that Jesus had to hide from the people on the mountain by himself because he perceived they were coming to make him the king of the Jews by force. The disciples were not with him, making it a more serious matter because he had to hide alone. To divert the people's attention from his hideout, the disciples entered the boat and sailed to Capernaum. The wind rose and blew the boat faster and further from Jesus, approximately 3-4 miles away. Jesus was later seen walking on water for 4 miles and almost reached the end of their journey to Capernaum because they arrived at their destination immediately after he got into the boat.

Walking on the sea for Jesus is the same as thinking possibilities for us. Thinking possibilities should therefore be a habit. You have to practice it on little things to get it into a format in your subconscious mind. Is it possible to live and think limitless? I perceive this is the only way to scale in life because life will always do what life does. Circumstances, situations, problems and challenges will always arise in business, family, and the workplace without an appointment. The antidote to failure is to thinking limitless.

You need to develop a limitless mindset by believing you can, you must and shall succeed. Say it loud to your hearing as many times as you can until the subconscious mind picks it up as a command. I can, I must, I shall! This won't be a quick fix like you have been taught that you shall have whatever you say. As much as it is true, this phenomenon did not factor in how many times you have to say it to get it because it depends on factors that are peculiar to individuals. The subconscious mind needs to receive the information as real before it can transmit the energy to attract what you are saying. When would the subconscious mind pick it up as real? I can never tell!

I believe limitless thinking is the art of inventors, achievers and frontiers of innovation. These are people who have learned to push their imagination beyond the limits. We do not have the same level of IQ, but we all have the mind which is all that is required for limitless thinking. It is time to open up the insight to wisdom in the next chapter. Please join me.

Part 3

WISDOM IN ACTION

Chapter 4

Discerning to Succeed

Life is a mystery until you understand the dynamics of God and life. We often talk about the miracle of getting a job, contract or visa, but we don't explain the work put into the achievement because it's more complex and difficult to explain the efforts made. This should not fool you into thinking there was no effort made because God loves partnership, even in performing miracles. We must pay attention to details in systems and structures for the achievement of success.

There are systems and structures in life. Let's be keen on understanding the systems, structures, of organisations we deal with to achieve success. It's time to wake up and give more attention to details. Therefore, understanding the system and structure of the institutions and organisations we deal with is crucial for success. The ability to discern when to apply faith and when to apply work is the difference between a goal-getter and a wishful thinker.

If I plant a seed in the ground, I have to wait for the process of germination to occur. There is an already laid-down system in the seed and in the soil to make it germinate. The seed is buried in the soil and remains inactive until certain conditions like water, light, or temperature trigger the germination. Science proved that. If these conditions are not met, the possibility of the seed dying is very high. For students at various levels, you need to understand what is required of you at the examination and what to do to achieve success. The same thing applies to people in business and on a job. Be curious enough to know the details of what is required in the organisation you are in. There is simply no benefit if you apply for a visa and don't read or meet the criteria set. There are criteria for almost everything in life. Your duty is to put your mind to the details and move into action on how to succeed in your endeavour. It is simply a waste of time and energy if you do not put your mind to details. That is how you discern to win if success is the goal. Knowing what works and what does not work and making the right choice. Every game has its rules. You cannot be a professional if you do not follow the rules. No matter how good you are on the basketball field, if you do not follow the rules, you will be disqualified. Therefore, those who master the rules of the game and perfect their skills make it to the top. Basically, the attention is on the detail, the rules, and the criteria needed to be observed, and that's how life works.

Wisdom, Knowledge and Understanding

Proverbs 3:19-20: The Lord, by wisdom, has founded the Earth; by understanding, has he established the heavens. By knowledge, the depths are broken up, and the clouds drop down the dew.

What is Knowledge?

Knowledge is the facts, information, and skills acquired through experience or education.

What is Understanding?

Understanding is the ability to have insight into the facts, information, and skills acquired through experience or education. {Understanding is the ability to have insight into knowledge.}

What Is Wisdom?

Wisdom is the correct application of facts, information, and skills acquired through experience or education. {Wisdom is the correct application of knowledge.}

I want you to see how knowledge, understanding, and wisdom are connected. When you know a thing and you understand it, then you can use it for your benefit; when you apply it that is wisdom. It all starts from knowledge. You are to give yourself the facts, information, and skills required. That's your job, and no one can do that except you open yourself or, better still, expose yourself to information. The ultimate goal is for you to be better than yesterday. Application of wisdom starts from receiving information, facts, and skills required. This makes you a high flyer and separates you from the rest.

Asking the Right Questions

Wisdom (application of insight, facts, information and skills required) usually asks the right questions. These questions stretch the mind to think out of the box to find solutions to problems. Questions help to define or find true intentions clouded by emotions, expectations of people and the force of pessimism.

"He who asks a question is a fool for 5 minutes; he who does not ask a question is a fool forever" - Chinese proverb.

What's the one thing that the world's leading innovators share with children? They both learn through asking questions.

"Successful people ask better questions, and as a result, they get better answers"

– Anthony Robbins.

Isaac Newton discovered 'gravity'; guess what his question was - "Why does an apple fall from a tree, but why does the moon not fall into the Earth?"

Solving Problems

Wisdom puts you ahead in problem-solving. The general approach to a problem is to lay back or ask for someone else to solve the problem. If you have read this book this far, you must tune your mind to be a problem solver. Get excited about problems. When you see a problem, your attitude should be to provide a solution. That is the mindset for success. This makes you aware of your environment on a larger scale and enlarges your scope of operation. Problem solvers are the ones who direct the course of the world. They impact significantly on what business should look like because if they create a car powered by a battery, then there has to be a charging centre. Problem solvers create a positive ripple effect. That's how societies are impacted, which then snowballs to states, countries, and nations. Join the ever-ready problem solvers; it's a club you cannot refuse.

Wisdom is the principal thing, and it starts with your exposure to information and awareness of your environment. Self-help online programs and books should be your delight. They equip you with the information and the skills you need to apply to solve certain problems. If you have to read to solve a particular problem, so be it. The stretch of your mind makes you better today than yesterday.

Having achieved success, what's next? Do you feel fulfilled and quit? The next chapter promises to answer most of the questions in your mind right now.

Chapter 5

Success Does Not Feel Successful

'So, the Jews said to the man who was cured, 'It is the Sabbath, it is not lawful for you to carry your pallet' (John 5:10).

This unnamed man had been ill for thirty-eight years, waiting for someone to push him into the pool, but nobody was willing to help him. The people of the city of Jerusalem actually knew he sat there, paralysed. Maybe some of them must have given him money to help him survive since he needs to eat and live even if he can't move around normally like every other human being. I would have thought there would be a shout that would make the king ask what was happening in the city near the pool when they saw this man walking, healed from his paralysed state. The opposite was the case with this man. They were quoting a law that says it is not lawful for him to carry his pallet on a Sunday.

For every success you achieve, there will always be new devils to fight. That's why success doesn't feel successful because you would have thought that is the end of the struggle. Success doesn't guarantee rest from all your trouble. Every achievement draws new critics and new supporters. You must be ready to deal with the challenges that come with success. I have heard successful people say it is easier to achieve success than to stay successful. Your definition of success must be completely clear to you. Be attached only to your mission and let that drive you as far as you can.

Today's world is full of people who think they know you more than you know yourself. So, they slide into your page on social media, trying to trend by criticising you. Be ready to face new challenges at every level. It will come in different forms. Be ready! If you make mistakes, correct them and move on. Do not allow anyone to deprive you of the mission and drive to keep striving. Success will not make everyone like you, so do not expect affection from people. If it shows up, embrace it, and if not, do not worry about it. Success is in various forms and categories. As long as you achieve your mission, that is success.

Success does not feel successful because when you conquer or achieve your goal, you create room for more. It never stops. There will be an expansion of ideas as you achieve success in your endeavours. As you climb the ladder of success, you see wider. There will always be room for more, so be ready because the goal you have now is not the ultimate. The goals you have set will have to be sustained after achievement, and then you will discover there is more to do. The first one million dollars is the hardest to make; after that, the next one gets easier, and you can't stop because you need more money as the vision and goals expand. Success is not a 100m race; it's a pursuit of a lifetime.

Have a Solid Mission Statement

A mission statement is a formal summary of the aims and values of a company, organisation or individual.

Here are some examples of corporate mission statements:

META: 'Build the future of human connection and the technology that makes it possible.'

AMAZON: 'To be Earth's most customer-centric company.'

GOOGLE: 'To organise the world's information and make it universally accessible and useful.'

Here is an example of a non-profit mission statement:

AMERICAN RED CROSS: 'To prevent and alleviate human suffering.'

Here are examples of a small business mission statement:

SUSTAINABLE FASHION BRAND: 'Designing eco-friendly clothing, promoting environmental responsibility.'

EDUCATION CONSULTING FIRM: 'Empowering students, guiding academic success.'

Here is an example from The Bible:

"The Spirit of the Lord is upon me because he has anointed me to preach good news to the poor, he has sent me to proclaim release to the captives and recovering of sight to the blind, to set at liberty those who are oppressed, to proclaim the acceptable year of the Lord"

– Luke 4:18.

a. To preach good news to the poor
b. To proclaim release to the captives
c. Recovery of sight for the blind
d. To set at liberty those who are oppressed
e. To proclaim the acceptable year of the Lord

Though his own did not receive him, Jesus Christ was focused on his mission. He was able to accomplish his mission despite the rejection he experienced to the point of death. That is what a mission statement does. It should keep you grounded and focused because there will certainly be attacks, opposition, critics, haters, and well-wishers, as well as room for expansion and sustenance. There will be days you might get tired and frustrated, but the mission statement will keep your drive on fire.

You need a mission statement that will keep your drive towards your goals. A mission statement will help you define purpose, provide direction towards your set goals and reduce distractions to the barest minimum. A mission statement will keep your eyes, heart and mind focused despite criticism, achievements and setbacks.

Your mission statement must certainly be the broad picture that shows your passion. Passion is a powerful force that cannot be easily stopped. Therefore, the mission statement is a description of your passion. If your passion is not expressed by the mission statement, then you are already a prey to the critics, and you may not find the drive to move on when the room for expansion is created. Criticism is not all bad in itself. Positive criticism can help you refocus, especially when you have good intentions, but the manner and way the intention was carried out could be wrong depending on culture, regulations, and standards. If a movement is not criticised, there should be a double check to know if the movement is impactful. I am saying, in essence, that criticism is one of the proofs of success. That is why your passion should be the main core of the mission statement. Stuff I cannot even imagine will be thrown at you depending on the impact you are making in your selected field. To keep going on in your line of pursuit will require passion.

Passion in essence, must be borne out of love for humanity. The problem you are trying to solve is not for machines; it is for human beings like you. In fact, it is love that creates a force of passion in you to solve the problem. It could be in entertainment, sports, media, the financial sector, artificial intelligence AI, security, communication, education, government and so on. Whatever you have passion for is your ministry. Your passion appoints you as a minister in your profession. That should give you the right and authority to go the whole length you need to stretch to achieve success. Just as Ministers are appointed by the President in a democratic government and given the powers to function in the best possible way to achieve the goals and objectives of the administration in power, so does passion appoints us, and love is basically the root of passion.

Therefore, as a Minister appointed by passion, professionalism, expertise, and good communication skills must be developed. You must keep the learning channels open for personal improvement, which will definitely translate to corporate improvement. Times change, and to remain relevant, we must adapt to the times and seasons as they come. Times and seasons should not erode our core values, but we must learn and relearn to keep up with the dynamic world we are living in.

I now officially welcome you to the beginning of your success stories as you practise the ideas written in this book. Welcome to the world of success.

All Bible verses are quoted from

The Revised Standard Version.

Email: oluwadamilare_durojaye@yahoo.com

LinkedIn: Dare Durojaye

Instagram: Dare Durojaye

Phone number: +234 808 209 1230

www.ingramcontent.com/pod-product-compliance
Lightning Source LLC
LaVergne TN
LVHW090128160826
845673LV00015B/1116

* 9 7 9 8 8 9 6 9 9 5 0 3 6 *